HAL LEONARD
UKULELE METHOD

AUDIO ACCESS INCLUDED

UKULELE FOR KIDS
METHOD & SONGBOOK

BY CHAD JOHNSON

Ukuleles featured in this book courtesy of Lanikai Ukuleles, a Hohner Company.

To access audio visit:
www.halleonard.com/mylibrary

Enter Code
2169-9623-3991-5126

ISBN 978-1-5400-0360-7

7777 W. BLUEMOUND RD. P.O. BOX 13819 MILWAUKEE, WI 53213

Visit Hal Leonard Online at
www.halleonard.com

𝅝 whole = 4 beats

𝅗𝅥 half = 2 beats

𝅘𝅥 quarter = 1 beat

𝅘𝅥𝅮 eighth = ½ beat

𝅘𝅥𝅯 sixteenth = ¼ beat

CONTENTS

METHOD

Selecting Your Ukulele......................4

Parts of the Ukulele 5

Holding the Ukulele 6

Hand Position 7

The C Chord 8

The F Chord............................9

Changing Chords 10

The C7 Chord 11

The A Minor Chord 12

The G Chord 14

The Note A 17

The Note B 18

The Note C 19

The Note E 20

The Note F 21

The Note G 22

Note Review...........................23

The B♭ Chord..........................25

The Notes C & D 28

Three-Four Time 29

The Note B♭ 29

The Shuffle Feel 30

The G Minor Chord 32

SONGBOOK

The Siamese Cat Song...................36

Supercalifragilisticexpialidocious 37

Riptide 38

I Still Haven't Found What I'm Looking For.........40

Up Around the Bend 42

How Much Is That Doggie in the Window 45

The Lion Sleeps Tonight..................46

Don't Worry, Be Happy 48

Stand by Me...........................50

I'm Yours.............................53

SELECTING YOUR UKULELE

Ukuleles mainly come in four sizes:

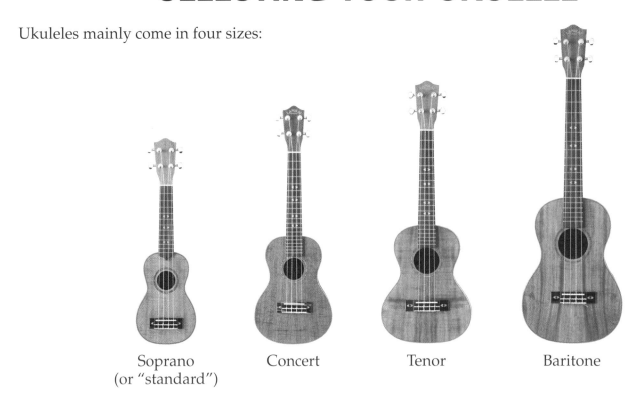

Soprano (or "standard")   Concert   Tenor   Baritone

Even a baritone ukulele isn't very big, but the soprano, concert, or tenor is probably best for a child to learn on. Pick the one that feels best to you.

Too Big   Good Fit

PARTS OF THE UKULELE

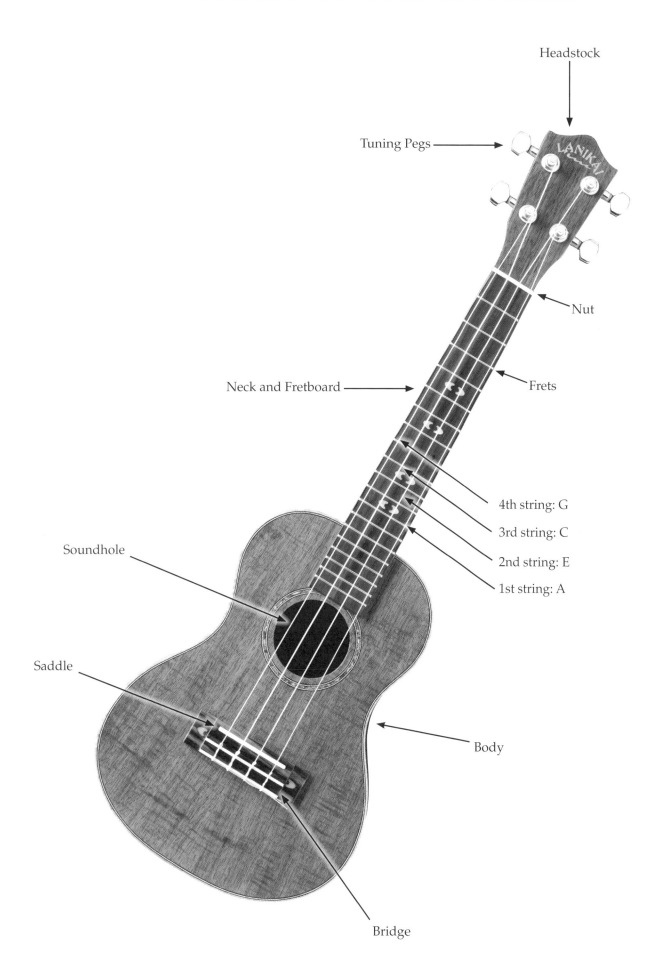

Headstock

Tuning Pegs

Nut

Neck and Fretboard

Frets

4th string: G

3rd string: C

2nd string: E

1st string: A

Soundhole

Saddle

Body

Bridge

Tuning

HOLDING THE UKULELE

There are many ways to hold a ukulele, both sitting and standing.

Sitting

- Sit up straight and relax your shoulders
- Place your feet flat on the floor or place one foot on a foot stool
- Tilt the neck of the ukulele slightly upwards
- Rest the ukulele on your leg or keep it in place by cradling it with your arm against your body

Wearing a Strap

Alternatively, you can wear a strap to keep your ukulele in place (sitting or standing). This will also allow the instrument to vibrate more freely and generally produce a bigger sound.

Standing

- Cradle the ukulele under the strumming arm to keep it in place
- Don't squeeze too tightly
- Tilt the neck of the ukulele slightly upwards

HAND POSITION

Left Hand

The fingers are numbered 1 through 4 (thumb is not numbered). Press the string down firmly between the two frets.

Place your thumb in the middle of the back of the neck and arch your fingers so that your palm doesn't touch the neck.

Right Hand

There are several ways to pluck or strum the strings of the ukulele. Most people strum the strings with either their extended first finger or thumb.

Some people prefer to play with a pick. Hold the pick between your thumb and first finger as shown in the photo and concentrating on using a downstroke to pick one string at a time.

THE C CHORD

Most people use the ukulele to play chords while they sing along. A **chord** is sounded when more than two strings are played at the same time. To play your first chord, C, use your 3rd finger to press the 3rd fret at the 1st string.

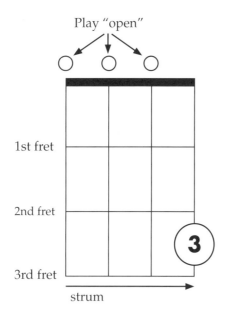

Music has a steady **beat**, like the ticking of a clock. Count aloud as you strum.

strum	strum	strum	strum		strum	strum	strum	strum
╱	╱	╱	╱		╱	╱	╱	╱
1	2	3	4		1	2	3	4

ARE YOU STRUMMING 🔊

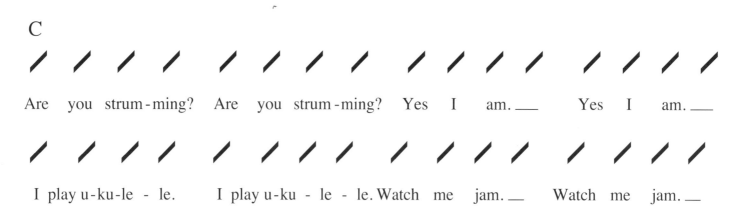

C

╱ ╱ ╱ ╱   ╱ ╱ ╱ ╱   ╱ ╱ ╱ ╱   ╱ ╱ ╱ ╱

Are you strum-ming? Are you strum-ming? Yes I am. ___ Yes I am. ___

╱ ╱ ╱ ╱   ╱ ╱ ╱ ╱   ╱ ╱ ╱ ╱   ╱ ╱ ╱ ╱

I play u-ku-le - le. I play u-ku - le - le. Watch me jam. ___ Watch me jam. ___

TEACHER MELODY:

THE F CHORD

For the F chord, we'll use two fingers. Use your 2nd finger to press the 4th string at the 2nd fret, and use your 1st finger to press the 2nd string at the 1st fret.

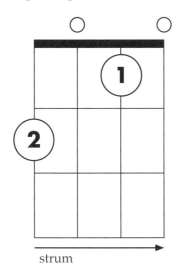

strum

Bar lines divide music into **measures**. A **double bar line** means the end.

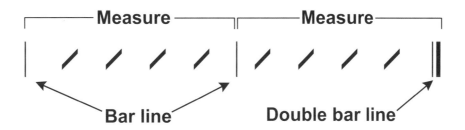

STRUM THE UKE

F

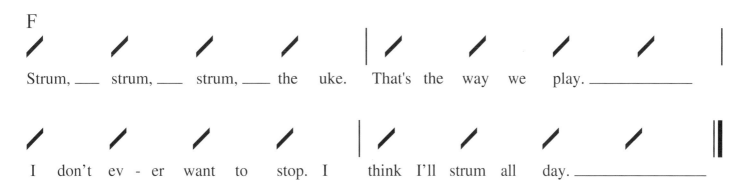

TEACHER MELODY:

9

CHANGING CHORDS

Practice strumming the F chord, and then change to the C chord.

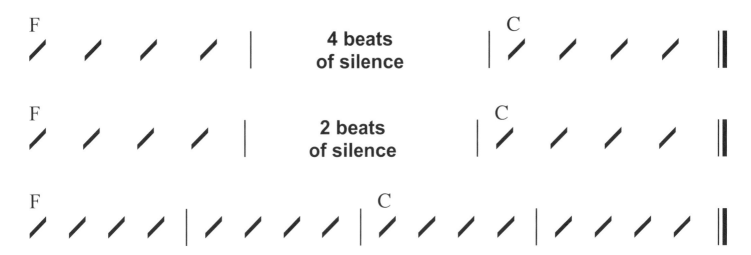

YELLOW SUBMARINE 🔊

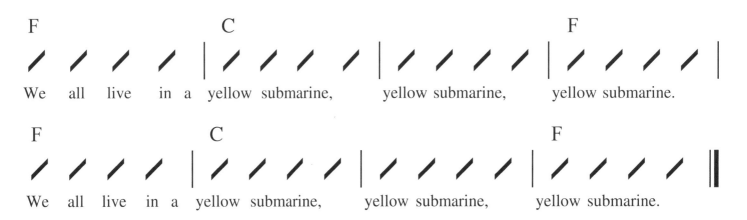

We all live in a yellow submarine, yellow submarine, yellow submarine.

We all live in a yellow submarine, yellow submarine, yellow submarine.

TEACHER ACCOMPANIMENT:

THE C7 CHORD

We can change one note from our C chord to make a C7 chord. Use your 1st finger to press the 1st string at the 1st fret.

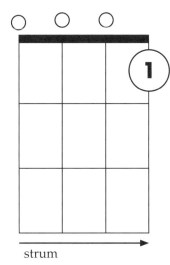

strum

THE HOKEY POKEY

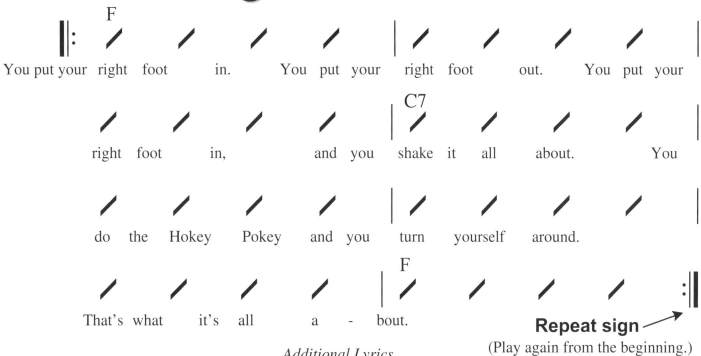

F

You put your right foot in. You put your right foot out. You put your

C7

right foot in, and you shake it all about. You

do the Hokey Pokey and you turn yourself around.

F

That's what it's all a - bout.

Repeat sign →
(Play again from the beginning.)

Additional Lyrics
Left foot
Right arm
Left arm
Whole self

Words and Music by Charles P. Macak, Tafft Baker and Larry LaPrise
Copyright © 1950 Sony/ATV Music Publishing LLC
Copyright Renewed
All Rights Administered by Sony/ATV Music Publishing LLC, 424 Church Street, Suite 1200, Nashville, TN 37219
International Copyright Secured All Rights Reserved

TEACHER MELODY:

THE A MINOR CHORD

Use your 2nd finger to press the 4th string at the 2nd fret.

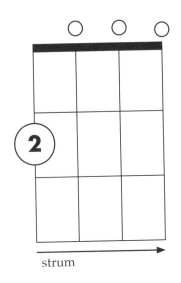

strum

RUN THROUGH THE JUNGLE

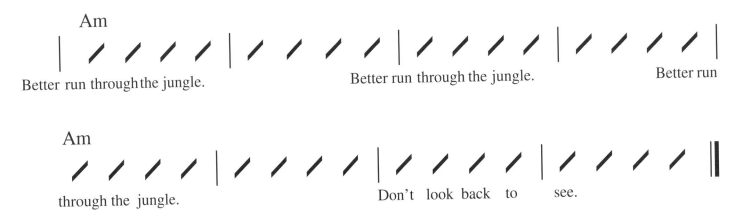

Am

Better run through the jungle.   Better run through the jungle.   Better run

Am

through the jungle.   Don't look back to   see.

Words and Music by John Fogerty
Copyright © 1970 Jondora Music c/o The Bicycle Music Company
Copyright Renewed
International Copyright Secured All Rights Reserved

TEACHER MELODY:

Switching between Am and F is really easy. Try it out in this Beatles song.

ELEANOR RIGBY

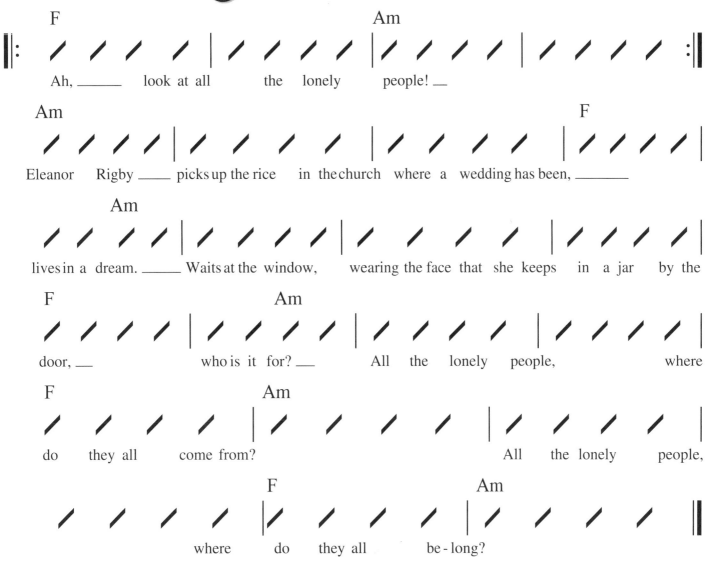

TEACHER MELODY:

THE G CHORD

For the G chord, you'll press three notes at the same time.

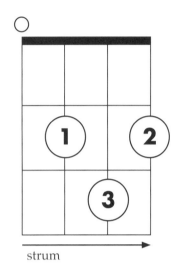

strum

Let's try changing between three chords you know.

C			F			G			C			
╱	╱	(don't play)	╱	╱	(don't play)	╱	╱	(don't play)	╱	╱	╱	╱
1	2	(3 4)	1	2	(3 4)	1	2	(3 4)	1	2	3	4

In this song, we'll be switching back and forth between G and F chords with no space in between.

WATCHIN' THE WAVES 🔊

TEACHER MELODY:

14

Now let's try our first songs with three different chords: C, F, and G.

THREE LITTLE BIRDS

Verse

C ⟋ ⟋ ⟋ ⟋ G ⟋ ⟋ ⟋ ⟋

Rise up this morning, smile with the rising sun. Three little birds

C ⟋ ⟋ ⟋ ⟋ F ⟋ ⟋ ⟋ ⟋

pitch by my doorstep, singing sweet

C ⟋ ⟋ ⟋ ⟋ G ⟋ ⟋ ⟋ ⟋

songs of melodies pure and true. Saying,

F ⟋ ⟋ ⟋ ⟋ C ⟋ ⟋ ⟋ ⟋

"This is my message to you."

Chorus

C ⟋ ⟋ ⟋ ⟋ ⟋ ⟋ ⟋ ⟋

Don't worry about a thing because

F ⟋ ⟋ ⟋ ⟋ C ⟋ ⟋ ⟋ ⟋

every little thing gonna be alright.

TEACHER MELODY:

Chords sometimes change in the middle of a measure too. Watch out for that in this next classic song by the Temptations.

AIN'T TOO PROUD TO BEG

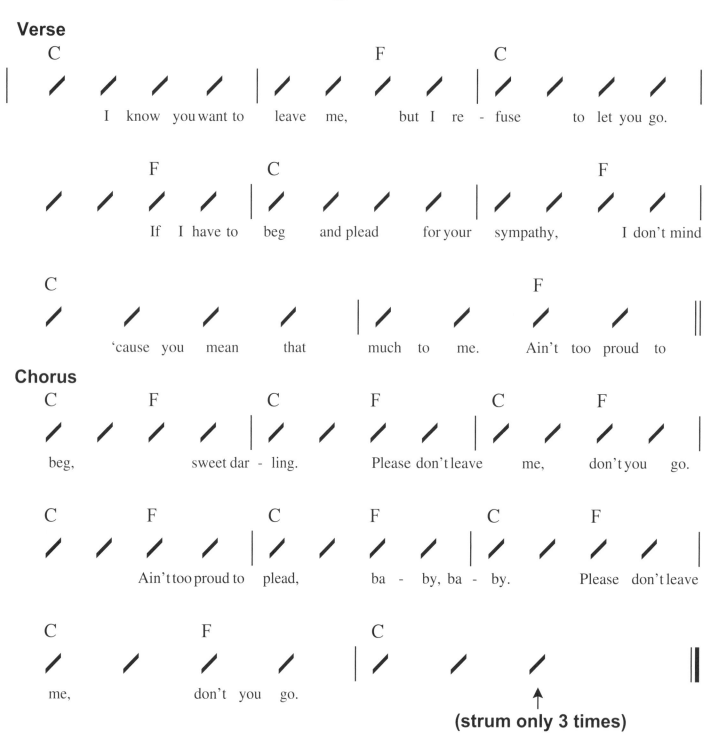

Verse

| C | | | | F | C |
I know you want to leave me, but I re - fuse to let you go.

F C F
If I have to beg and plead for your sympathy, I don't mind

C F
'cause you mean that much to me. Ain't too proud to

Chorus

C F C F C F
beg, sweet dar - ling. Please don't leave me, don't you go.

C F C F C F
Ain't too proud to plead, ba - by, ba - by. Please don't leave

C F C
me, don't you go.

(strum only 3 times)

Words and Music by Edward Holland Jr. and Norman Whitfield
Copyright © 1966 Jobete Music Co., Inc.
Copyright Renewed
All Rights Administered by Sony/ATV Music Publishing LLC on behalf of Stone Agate Music (A Division of Jobete Music Co., Inc.), 424 Church Street, Suite 1200, Nashville, TN 37219
International Copyright Secured   All Rights Reserved

TEACHER MELODY:

16

THE NOTE A

So far, you have learned to play chords. If you remember, a chord is sounded when you play more than two strings together. Now let's play some single notes. This is the way we play melodies on the ukulele.

To play the A note, pluck the 1st string open with your finger, thumb, or pick.

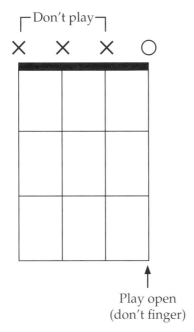

Don't play

Play open (don't finger)

Music is written on a **staff** of five lines and four spaces. Each line or space is assigned a letter name. A **clef** appears at the beginning of every staff. Ukulele music is written on a **treble clef**.

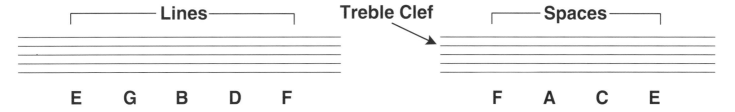

Lines — Treble Clef — **Spaces**

E G B D F   F A C E

Our open 1st string is the note A, which is the second space up on the staff. Play each A note slowly and evenly.

MALAGUEÑA

TEACHER ACCOMPANIMENT:

THE NOTE B

Use your 2nd finger to press the 1st string at the 2nd fret.

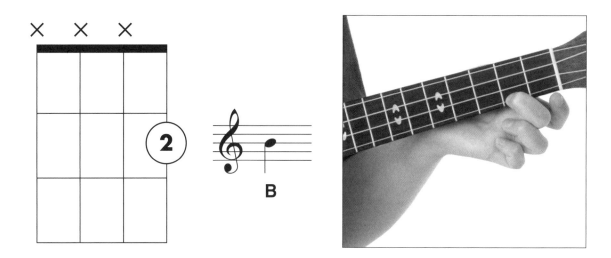

A **time signature** appears at the beginning of a piece of music. It tells how many beats are in each measure and what kind of note is counted as one beat. In 4/4 ("four-four") time, there are four beats in each measure, and a **quarter note** is counted as one beat. It has a solid notehead and a stem (♩).

TWO NOTE JAM

Count: 1   2   3   4

TEACHER ACCOMPANIMENT:

FLOATIN' ON THE WAVES 🔊

TEACHER ACCOMPANIMENT:

THE NOTE C

Use your 3rd finger to press the 3rd fret on the 1st string.

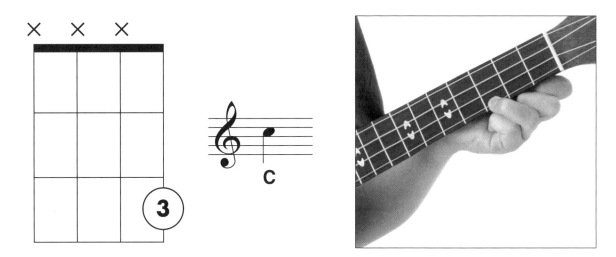

A **half note** (♩) lasts twice as long as a quarter note; it gets two beats.

SEASICK 🔊

Count: 1 - 2 3 4

TEACHER ACCOMPANIMENT:

STAIRCLIMBING 🔊

TEACHER ACCOMPANIMENT:

THE NOTE E

Now let's move on to the 2nd string. To play the note E, pluck the 2nd string open.

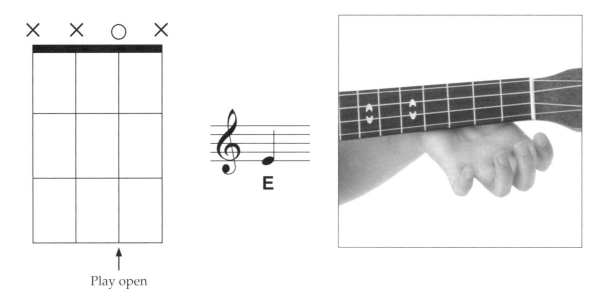

Play open

A **whole note** (𝅝) is twice as long as a half note or four times as long as a quarter note. It lasts four beats, or a whole measure in 4/4 time.

THE UKE BLUES 🔊

Count: 1 2 3 4   1 - 2 - 3 - 4

TEACHER ACCOMPANIMENT:

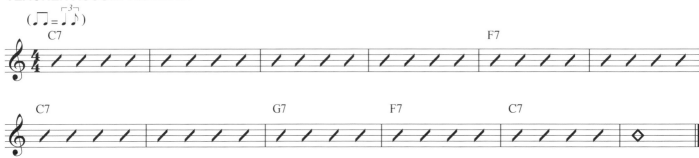

20

THE NOTE F

Use your 1st finger to press the 2nd string at the 1st fret.

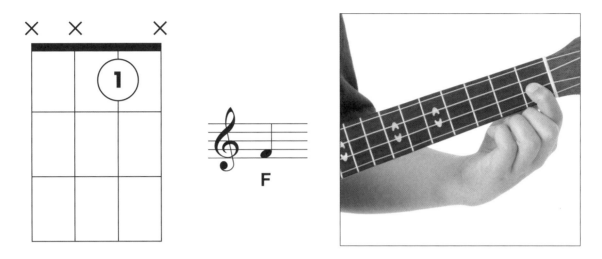

Rests are beats of silence. The **quarter note rest** (𝄽) means to be silent for one beat. Try counting silently when you see a rest.

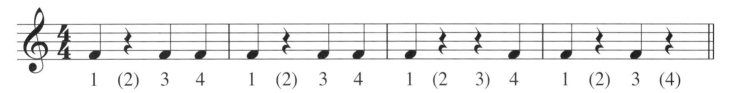

1 (2) 3 4   1 (2) 3 4   1 (2 3) 4   1 (2) 3 (4)

STOP AND GO 🔊

TEACHER ACCOMPANIMENT:

21

THE NOTE G

Use your 3rd finger to press the 2nd string at the 3rd fret.

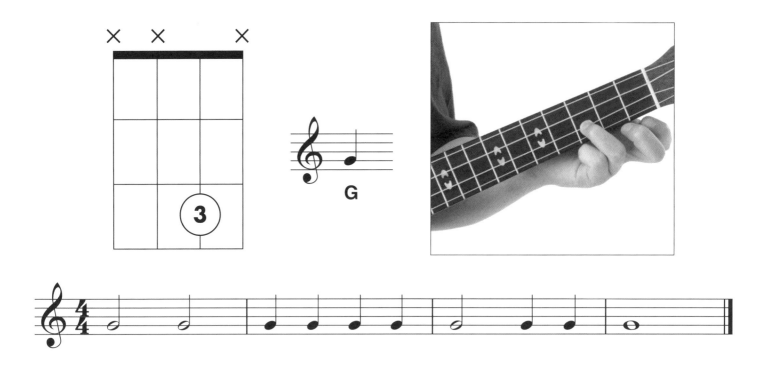

A **half note rest** (–) means to be silent for two beats.

HILL CLIMBING

TEACHER ACCOMPANIMENT:

Try this example with half note rests and quarter note rests. Remember to count!

1 (2) 3 4   1 2 (3 4)   1 2 3 (4)   1 (2) 3 4

NOTE REVIEW

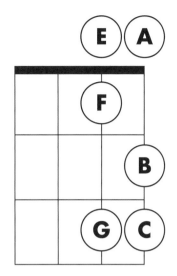

E   F   G   A   B   C

The notes in the following exercises move from string to string. As you are playing one note, look ahead to the next and get your fingers in position.

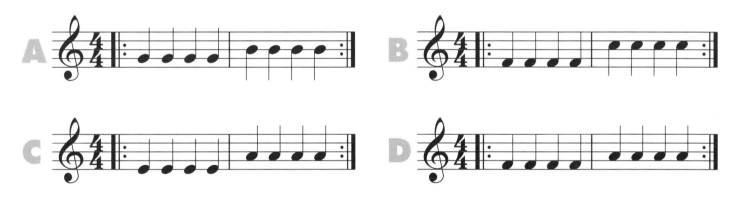

WINDCHIMES 🔊

TEACHER ACCOMPANIMENT:

Some songs begin with **pickup notes**. Count the missing beats out loud before you start playing.

ISLAND STREAM

Teacher plays chord symbols

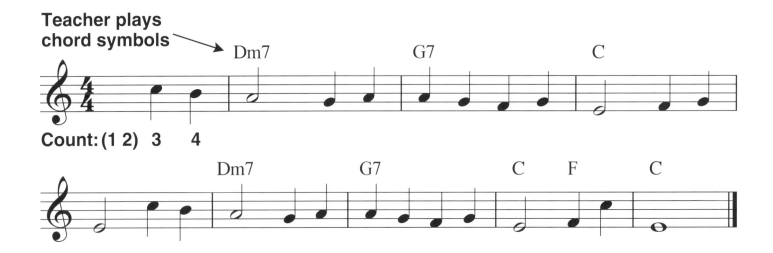

SHE LOVES YOU

Teacher plays chord symbols

Words and Music by John Lennon and Paul McCartney
Copyright © 1963 by NORTHERN SONGS LIMITED
Copyright Renewed
All rights for the U.S.A., its territories and possessions and Canada assigned to and controlled by GIL MUSIC CORP., 1650 Broadway, New York, NY 10019
International Copyright Secured   All Rights Reserved

THE B♭ CHORD

For the B♭ chord, you'll need to press down all four strings. Lay your 1st finger down across both the 1st and 2nd strings.

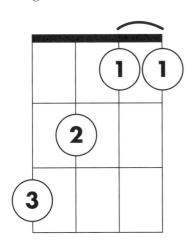

Strum marks are sometimes written on the staff to help you keep track of where the strums are within the measure.

THIS LAND IS YOUR LAND

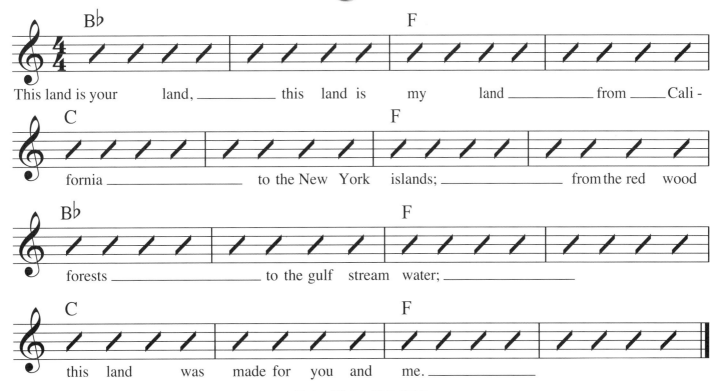

This land is your land, _____ this land is my land _____ from ____ Cali-
fornia _____ to the New York islands; _____ from the red wood
forests _____ to the gulf stream water; _____
this land was made for you and me. _____

TEACHER MELODY:

A **whole note rest** (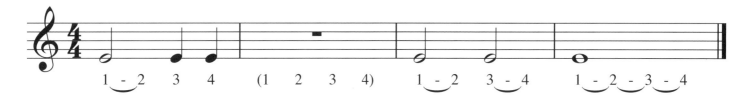) means to be silent for four beats, or a whole measure.

1 - 2   3   4   (1   2   3   4)   1 - 2   3 - 4   1 - 2 - 3 - 4

BARBARA ANN

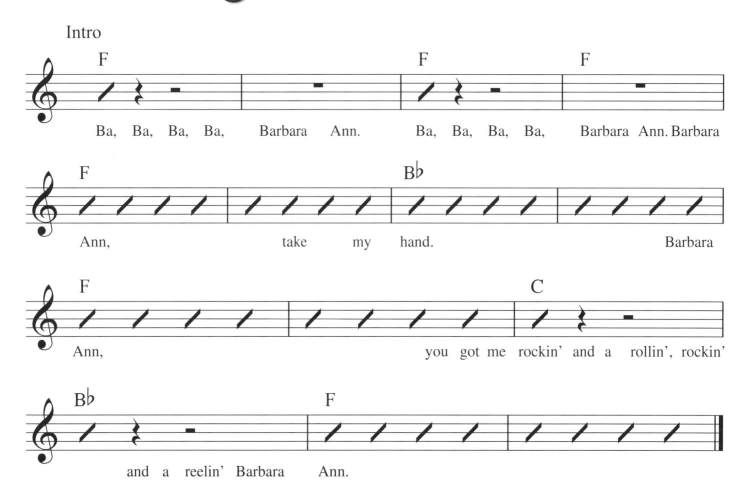

Intro

F   F   F

Ba, Ba, Ba, Ba,   Barbara Ann.   Ba, Ba, Ba, Ba,   Barbara Ann. Barbara

F   Bb

Ann,   take   my   hand.   Barbara

F   C

Ann,   you got me rockin' and a   rollin', rockin'

Bb   F

and a reelin' Barbara   Ann.

Words and Music by Fred Fassert
Copyright © 1959 EMI Longitude Music and Cousins Music Inc.
Copyright Renewed
All Rights Administered by Sony/ATV Music Publishing LLC, 424 Church Street, Suite 1200, Nashville, TN 37219
International Copyright Secured   All Rights Reserved

TEACHER MELODY:

So far, you have played four downstrokes for each measure. Now let's strum twice for every beat, or eight times for each measure. Alternate between downstrums and upstrums.

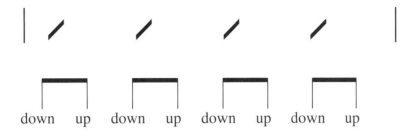

down   up   down   up   down   up   down   up

MR. TAMBOURINE MAN 🔊

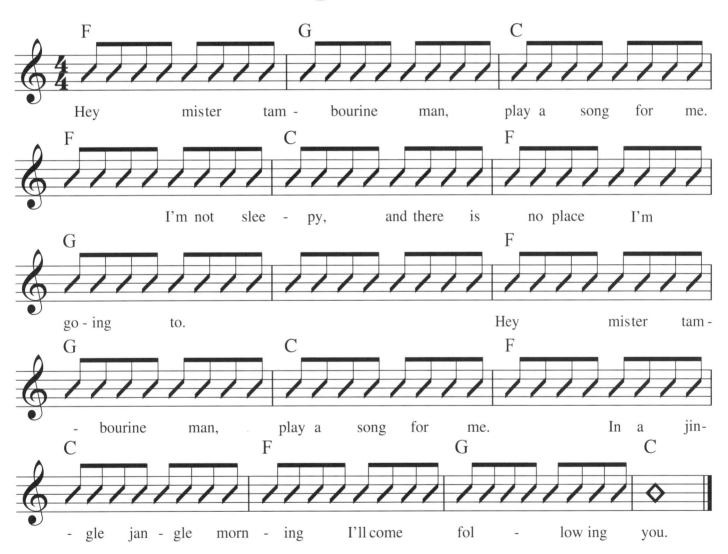

TEACHER MELODY:

THE NOTES C & D

You already learned how to play the note C on the 1st string. Another (lower) C note can be played by plucking the 3rd string open. To play the D note, press the 3rd string at the 2nd fret.

ETUDE 🔊

Teacher plays chord symbols

THREE-FOUR TIME

Some music has three beats per measure instead of four. The symbol for three-four time is:

 Three beats per measure; quarter note (♩) gets one beat.

AMAZING GRACE

Teacher plays chord symbols

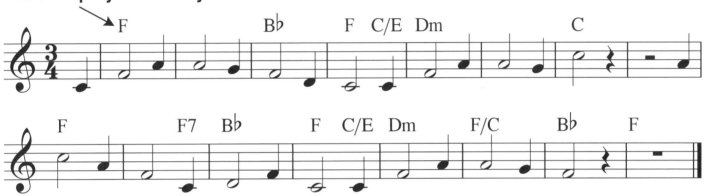

THE NOTE B♭

We have one more note we'll learn. Use your 1st finger to press the 1st string at the 1st fret.

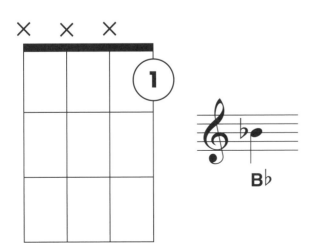

BIRTHDAY SONG

Teacher plays chord symbols

LOVE ME TENDER

Teacher plays chord symbols

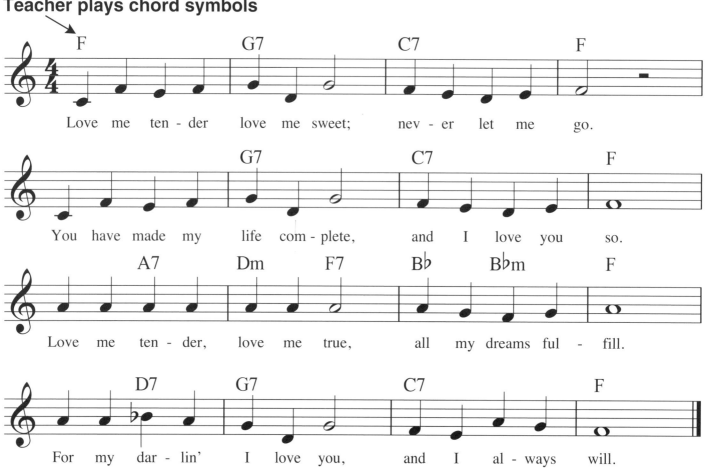

Love me ten - der, love me sweet; nev - er let me go.

You have made my life com - plete, and I love you so.

Love me ten - der, love me true, all my dreams ful - fill.

For my dar - lin' I love you, and I al - ways will.

THE SHUFFLE FEEL

Many songs are played with a **shuffle feel**. This means that the eighth notes sound lopsided; the first one in each beat is longer than the second one. The symbol for the shuffle feel is:

Listen to the audio to hear how this sounds on a C chord. First, the chord will be strummed normally; then you'll hear a shuffle feel.

Shuffle Feel

Now try playing "Rock Around the Clock" with a shuffle feel.

ROCK AROUND THE CLOCK

Intro

F

One, two three o'clock, four o'clock rock. Five, six, seven o'clock,

eight o'clock rock. Nine, ten, eleven o'clock, twelve o'clock rock. We're gonna

Verse
F

rock a-round the clock tonight. Put your glad rags on and

join me hon. We'll have some fun when the clock strikes one. We're gonna

Bb

rock around the clock tonight. We're gonna rock, rock, rock, 'til the

C

broad daylight. We're gonna rock, gonna rock a-

Bb   F

round the clock tonight.

Words and Music by Max C. Freedman and Jimmy DeKnight
Copyright © 1953 Myers Music Inc., Kassner Associated Publishers Ltd. and Capano Music
Copyright Renewed
All Rights on behalf of Myers Music Inc. and Kassner Associated Publishers Ltd. Administered by Sony/ATV Music Publishing LLC, 424 Church Street, Suite 1200, Nashville, TN 37219
International Copyright Secured   All Rights Reserved

TEACHER MELODY:

F

etc.

THE G MINOR CHORD

Let's learn one more chord. For the G minor chord, you'll need to press three strings at the same time.

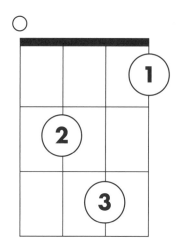

Practice alternating the G minor chord with the other chords you've learned, and then try it out in our last song: "Surfer Girl."

SURFER GIRL

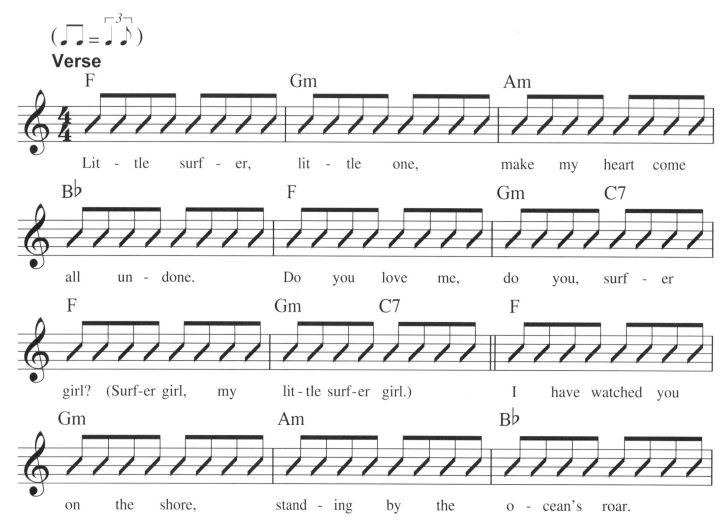

Words and Music by Brian Wilson
Copyright © 1962 BMG Bumblebee
Copyright Renewed
All Rights Administered by BMG Rights Management (US) LLC
All Rights Reserved   Used by Permission

Bridge

Verse

TEACHER MELODY:

CERTIFICATE OF ACHIEVEMENT

Congratulations to

_____

(YOUR NAME)

_____

(DATE)

You have completed

UKULELE FOR KIDS

_____

(TEACHER SIGNATURE)

You are now ready for

HAL LEONARD UKULELE METHOD BOOK 1

UKULELE FOR KIDS SONGBOOK

THE SIAMESE CAT SONG

from *LADY AND THE TRAMP*

Words and Music by Peggy Lee
and Sonny Burke

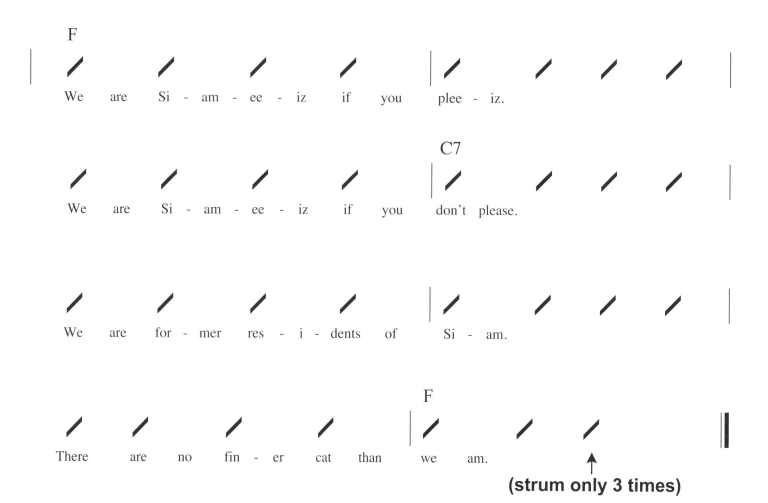

F

We are Si - am - ee - iz if you plee - iz.

C7

We are Si - am - ee - iz if you don't please.

We are for - mer res - i - dents of Si - am.

F

There are no fin - er cat than we am.

(strum only 3 times)

TEACHER MELODY:

SUPERCALIFRAGILISTICEXPIALIDOCIOUS

from MARY POPPINS

Words and Music by Richard M. Sherman
and Robert B. Sherman

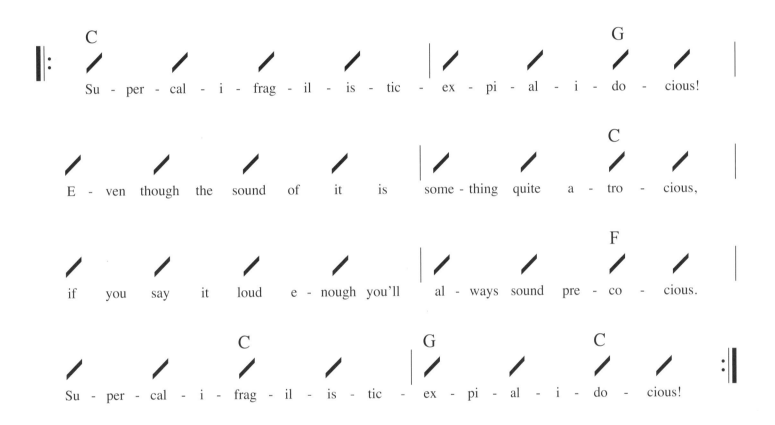

TEACHER MELODY:

RIPTIDE

Words and Music by
Vance Joy

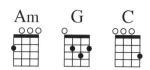

Am   G   C

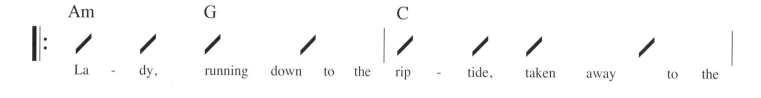

Am   **G**   **C**

La - dy, running down to the rip - tide, taken away to the

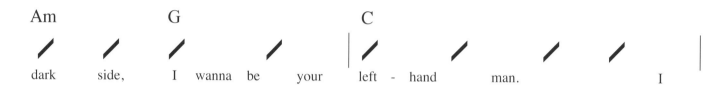

Am   **G**   **C**

dark side, I wanna be your left - hand man. I

Am   **G**   **C**

love you when you're sing - ing that song, and I got a lump in my

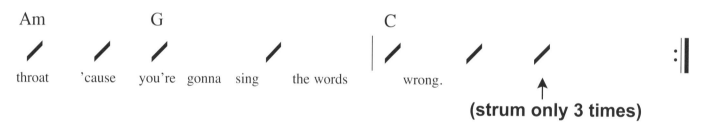

Am   **G**   **C**

throat 'cause you're gonna sing the words wrong.

(strum only 3 times)

TEACHER MELODY:

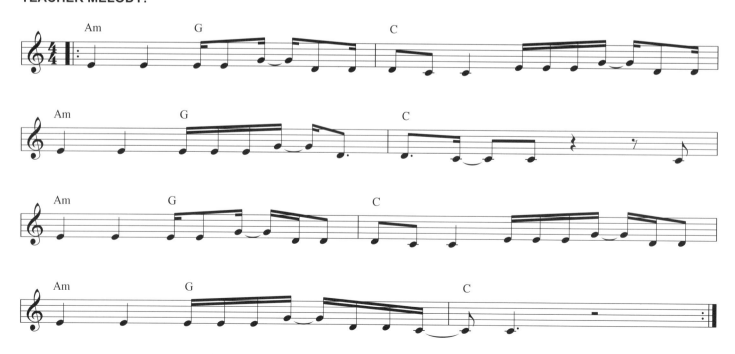

This page is intentionally left blank to avoid an unnecessary page turn.

I STILL HAVEN'T FOUND WHAT I'M LOOKING FOR

Words and Music by
U2

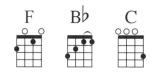

Verse

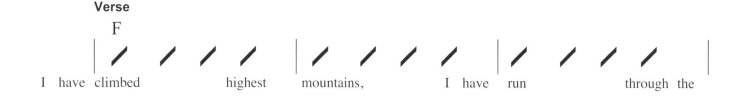

I have climbed highest mountains, I have run through the

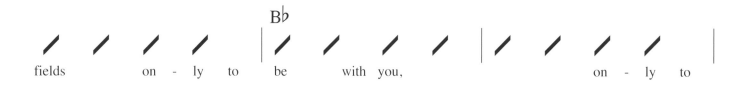

fields on - ly to be with you, on - ly to

be with you. I have run, I have

TEACHER MELODY:

(strum only 3 times)

UP AROUND THE BEND

Words and Music by
John Fogerty

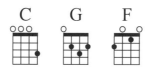

Verse

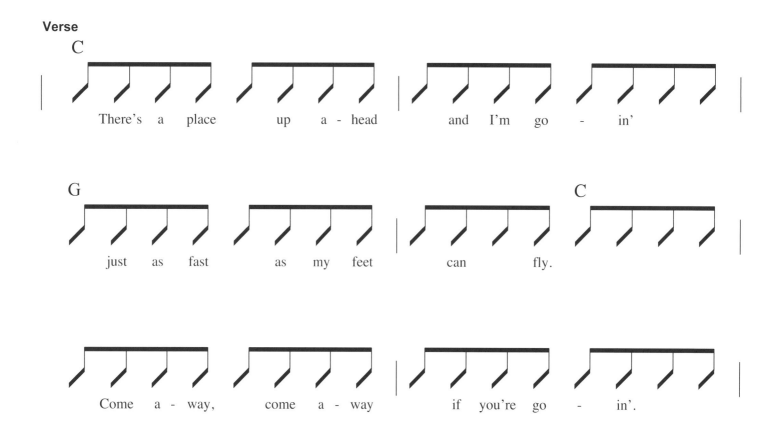

There's a place up a - head and I'm go - in'

just as fast as my feet can fly.

Come a - way, come a - way if you're go - in'.

TEACHER MELODY:

G   C

Leave the sink - in' ship   be - hind.

Chorus

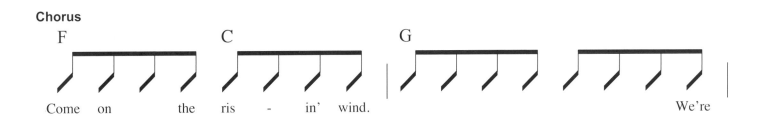

F   C   G

Come on the ris - in' wind.   We're

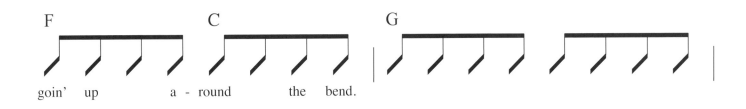

F   C   G

goin' up a - round the bend.

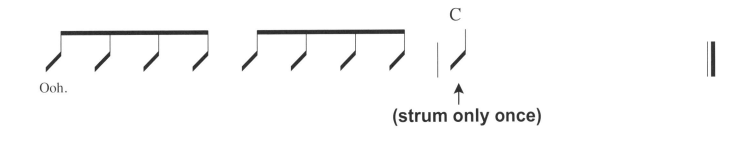

C

Ooh.

(strum only once)

This page is intentionally left blank to avoid an unnecessary page turn.

HOW MUCH IS THAT DOGGIE IN THE WINDOW

Words and Music by
Bob Merrill

TEACHER MELODY:

THE LION SLEEPS TONIGHT

New Lyrics and Revised Music by
George David Weiss, Hugo Peretti
and Luigi Creatore

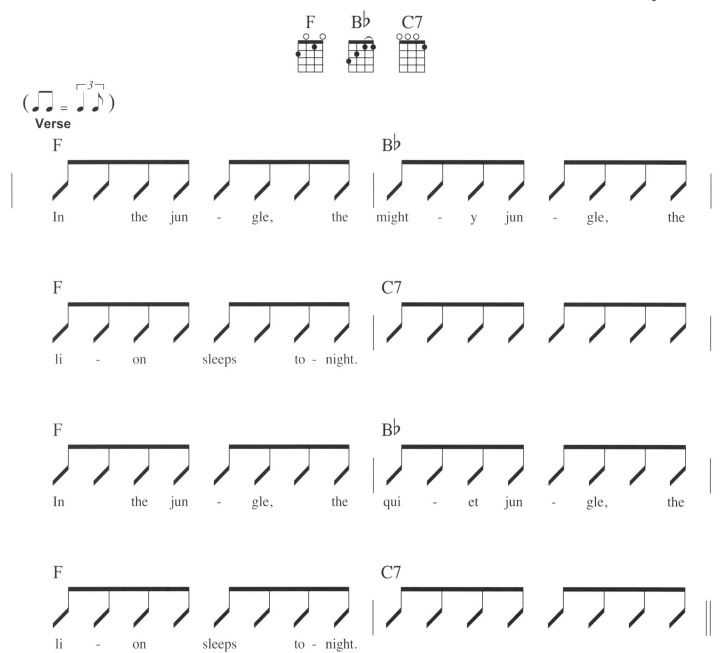

TEACHER MELODY:

Chorus

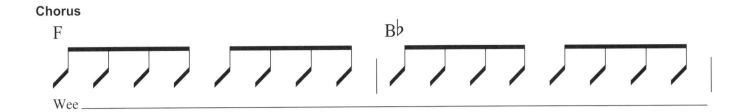

Wee _____

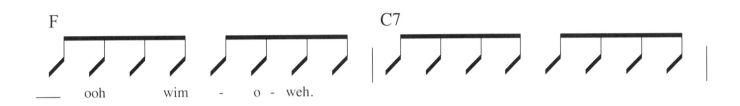

___ ooh wim - o - weh.

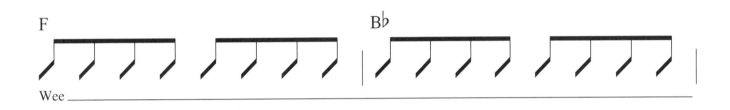

Wee _____

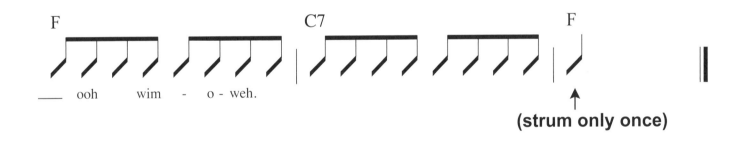

___ ooh wim - o - weh. **(strum only once)**

47

DON'T WORRY, BE HAPPY

Words and Music by
Bobby McFerrin

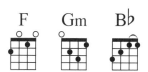

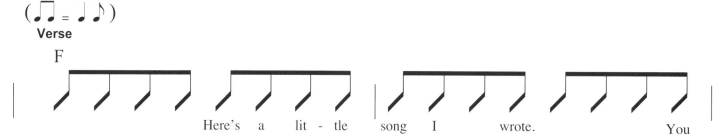

Here's a lit - tle song I wrote. You

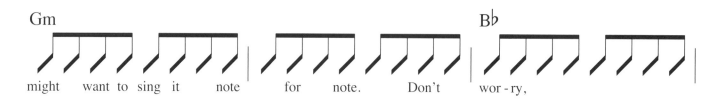

might want to sing it note for note. Don't wor - ry,

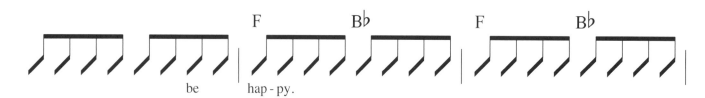

be hap - py.

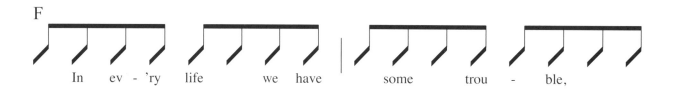

In ev - 'ry life we have some trou - ble,

TEACHER MELODY:

STAND BY ME

Words and Music by Jerry Leiber,
Mike Stoller and Ben E. King

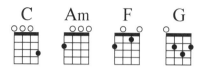

Verse

When the night   has come

and the land is dark,   and the moon

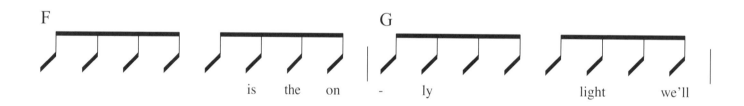

is the on - ly   light we'll

TEACHER MELODY:

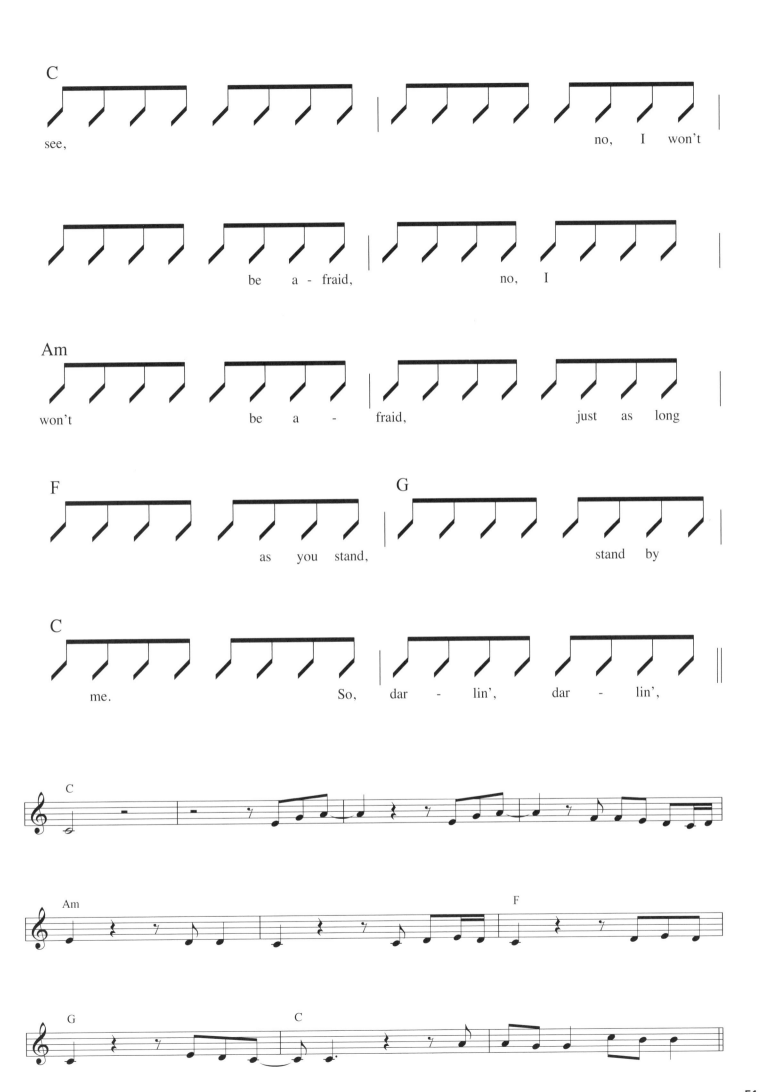

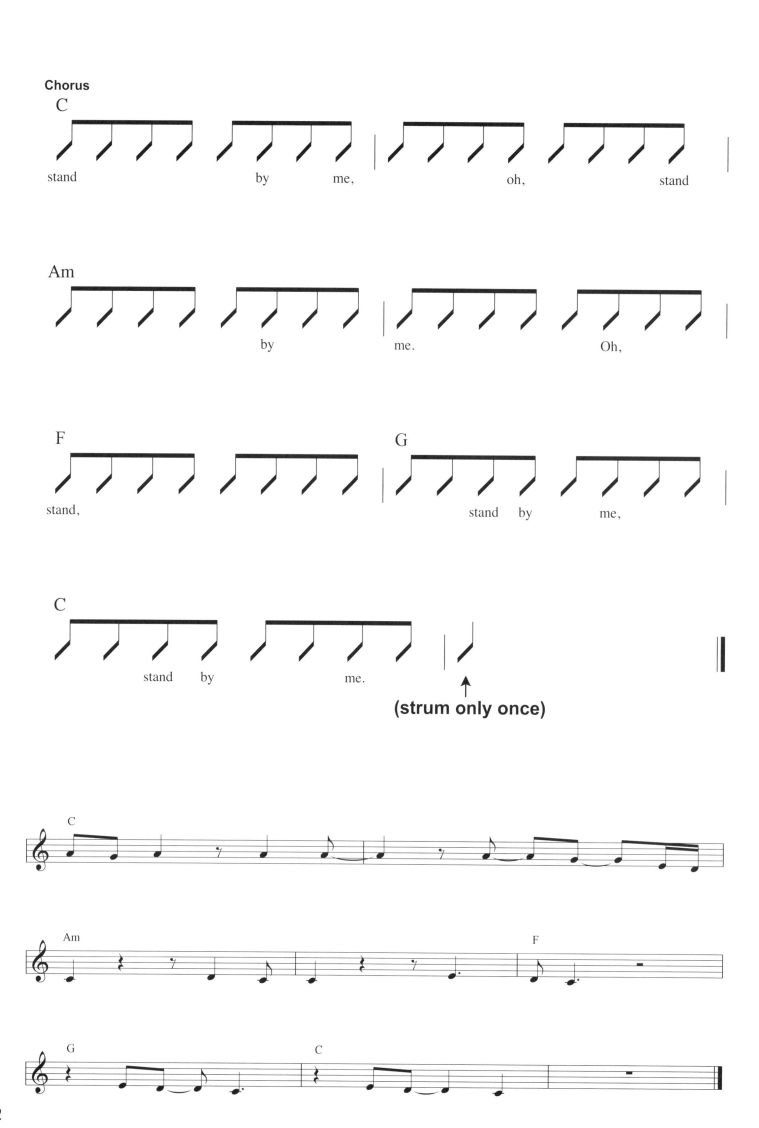

Chorus

I'M YOURS

Words and Music by
Jason Mraz

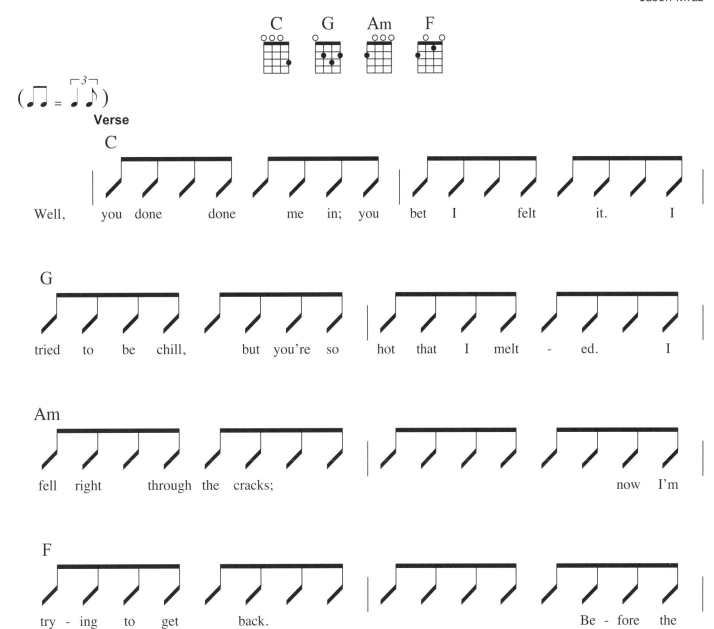

TEACHER MELODY:

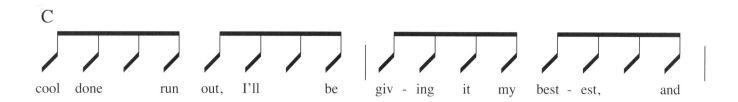

C

cool done run out, I'll be giv - ing it my best - est, and

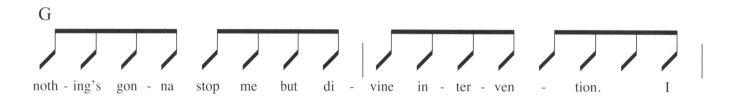

G

noth - ing's gon - na stop me but di - vine in - ter - ven - tion. I

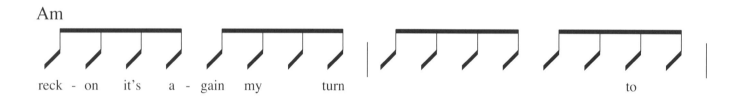

Am

reck - on it's a - gain my turn to

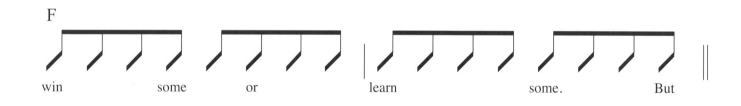

F

win some or learn some. But